W9-CMG-926

# Microlife That Rots Things

Steve Parker

Chicago, Illinois

© 2006 Raintree
Published by Raintree
A division of Reed Elsevier Inc.
Chicago, IL

All rights reserved. No part of this publication may be reproduced or transmitted in any form or by any means, electronic or mechanical, including photography, recording, taping, or any information storage and retrieval system, without permission in writing from the publisher.

For information, address the publisher:
Raintree, 100 N. LaSalle, Suite 1200
Chicago, IL 60602
Customer Service  888-363-4266
Visit our website at www.raintreelibrary.com

Printed and bound in China by South China Printing Company Ltd
10 09 08 07 06
10 9 8 7 6 5 4 3 2 1

Edited by Katie Orchard
Designed by Tim Mayer
Picture Research by Lynda Lines and Frances Bailey
Production by Duncan Gilbert

Library of Congress Cataloging-in-Publication Data
Parker, Steve.
  Microlife that rots things / Steve Parker
    p. cm. -- (The amazing world of microlife)
  Includes bibliographical references and index.
  ISBN 1-4109-1848-3 (lib. bdg. : hardcover) --
  ISBN 1-4109-1853-X (pbk.)
1. Pathogenic microorganisms--Juvenile literature.
2. Scavengers (Zoology)--Juvenile literature  I. Title.
II. Series: Parker, Steve. Amazing world of microlife

QH530.5.P37 2005
577'.16--dc22

2005004226

## Acknowledgments

The publishers would like to thank the following for permission to reproduce photographs: Corbis p. **4** (David Muench); NHPA p. **16** (David Middleton); OSF/photolibrary.com pp. **8** (E. R. Degginger), **20**; photolibrary.com pp. **11** (Mona Lisa Production), **14**, **15**; Science Photo Library pp. **1** (Manfred Kage), **3** (Eye of Science), **5** (Eye of Science), **7** (Eye of Science), **9** (Dr. Jeremy Burgess), **10** (Eye of Science), **12** (Dr. Jeremy Burgess), **17** (Eye of Science), **18** (Manfred Kage), **19** (David Scharf), **22** (Dr. Jeremy Burgess), **23** (Andrew Syred), **24** (Susumu Nishinaga), **25** (Jeff Lepore), **26** (Eye of Science), **27** (David Scharf), **28** (George Lepp/Agstock); Still Pictures pp. **6** (David Cavagnaro), **13** (Martin Harvey); Topfoto pp. **21** (Steve Warmowski/Journal-Courier/The Image Works), **29** (Jack K. Clark/The Image Works).

Cover photograph of termites feeding on wood reproduced with permission of Science Photo Library (Eye of Science).

Every effort has been made to contact copyright holders of any material reproduced in this book. Any omissions will be rectified in subsequent printings if notice is given to the publishers.

The paper used to print this book comes from sustainable resources.

j  JUN 0 1 2006
579
Pur
Mt. Lebanon Public Library
Children's Library

# Contents

Some words are shown in bold, **like this**. You can find out what they mean by looking in the Glossary.

# What a Lot of Rot!

What happens to old, dead plants and animals? They lie around on the ground—but not for long. Over time, they go moldy and rotten, turning into crumbly pieces or smelly goo. Finally, they break into tiny bits too small to see, which go into the soil. This whole process is called rotting or **decay**.

This old log is slowly rotting into the soil. Millions of living things, from worms and **grubs** to tiny bugs, are making it rot.

This tiny rotter is called a roundworm. It would fit onto the period at the end of this sentence. A microscope shows it as larger than a finger.

# The microrotters

Rotting is done by living things. Many "rotters" are so tiny that we need a magnifying glass, or even a **microscope**, to see them. This book tells the story of the microrotters. Their world is dirty and smelly—but we need them. Without them, we would be knee-deep in old bits of plants and animals, which would not have rotted away.

# A Heap of Rotters

In a huge jungle, there are many kinds of animals, from mice and monkeys to tigers and elephants. When we put old leaves, grass, and leftover food on a **compost heap**, we make a "mini-jungle." Many creatures live in a compost heap, but most are too small to see. Some munch bits of plants while others are fierce hunters.

Many people put old leaves, twigs, and other garden material onto a compost heap. This helps natural recycling.

**WHAT DOES NOT ROT**
Substances we make in factories, such as glass, metal, and plastic, do not rot. They last for thousands of years. So we should put them in recycling bins so they can be used again.

# Back to soil

In a compost heap, tiny animals and other microlife gradually turn once-living things into soil. The soil is rich in food for growing new plants. Rotting is nature's way of using things again and again. It is natural recycling.

Microrotters include frilly- and tube-shaped **bacteria**.

# The Rot Sets In

When old things start to rot, minibeasts soon move in.
They chew and chomp as they feed. They break up
soft things such as flowers and fruit very quickly.
Hard things such as bark and wood take longer.
But minibeasts never stop nibbling.

## WOODWORM

Sometimes small, wormlike grubs, called woodworm, eat wood in houses and furniture. Then they turn into beetles, come out of the wood, and fly away. They leave small holes in the wood where they come out.

As beetle grubs eat wood, they leave a pattern of tunnels.

Pill bugs chew damp wood and soon turn it into a soft powder.

## Munching minibeasts

Minibeast rotters include earwigs, pill bugs, millipedes, as well as the **grubs** (young) of beetles, ants, and other insects. As they eat, pieces of food fall out of their mouths—like the crumbs when we eat cake and cookies. These pieces do not go to waste. They are food for even smaller rotters!

# Nests for Rotters

Termites and some ants eat old wood with their tiny, pincer-like mouths. They make tunnels and nests inside the wood. Termites and ants can chew through wooden furniture, houses, and even bridges, until they collapse in a heap of powder.

Termites scurry through their tunnels, chewing bits of rotting wood.

This building has been destroyed by termites.

## Moldy food

Other termites and ants make nests in soil. They take old leaves, twigs, flowers, and small dead animals to the nest. As these things become **moldy** and rotten, the termites and ants feed on them.

**A LOT OF EGGS**

Only one termite in a nest lays eggs—the queen. She can lay 1,000 eggs every day for ten years!

# Rotten Meat

Animals die all the time. Fish and frogs, elephants and eagles—no creature lives forever. When a creature dies, the rotters move in. Flies lay their eggs on the dead body. The eggs quickly hatch into **maggots**, which eat into the rotting flesh. Beetles lay their eggs, too. Out of the eggs hatch **grubs**.

**KEEP FOOD CLEAN**
Flies spread microrotters and germs onto our food. We should keep our meat covered and clean, and make sure it is properly cooked.

Maggots have no eyes, legs, or feelers. They turn into adult flies.

# Meat and bones

As maggots and grubs eat, they leave behind bits of half-chewed meat. They also leave droppings. These droppings are food for more rotters. Soon, the dead animal's body is mostly **decayed** and gone, with just the hard bones left behind. Even these bones crumble into the soil after a long time.

The body of this warthog (a type of wild pig) is gradually rotting into the mud.

# Waste Not, Want Not

Animals do not use toilets. They leave their waste droppings, or dung, on the ground. Droppings smell horrible to us. But they smell wonderful to many tiny creatures, such as flies and beetles. These minirotters rush to the fresh piles of droppings and eat them!

The dung beetle rolls dung into a ball and lays eggs on it. When the grubs hatch, they eat the dung.

**PLENTY OF DUNG**
One elephant produces over 265 pounds (120 kilograms) of droppings every day. That is the weight of two adult people—and enough to feed 3,000 dung beetles!

Piles of fresh dung such as cow pats are food for hungry flies and beetles.

## A smelly meal

Droppings contain bits of leftover food. So minirotters have a great feast. Some kinds of flies and beetles lay their eggs on the droppings. The eggs hatch into **maggots** and **grubs**, which also feed on the smelly meal. Soon, the droppings are broken up and are gone.

# Mite Decay

A bucketful of soil contains thousands of **mites**. Mites are tiny, eight-legged cousins of spiders. They chew the munched-up leftovers from bigger creatures, including bits of old leaves, flowers, fruit, and twigs. As they feed, they make even smaller leftovers, which help the rot and **decay**.

**MITES EAT MITES!** Many kinds of mites eat old, rotting bits of plants and animals. But they are always in danger—from other kinds of mites, which try to eat them!

Millions of mites live in the layer of needle leaves under **conifer** trees such as pines and firs.

Turtle mites have hard, rounded shells, like a turtle's shell.

## Cool and damp

Most mites live in **leaf litter**. This is the layer of dead leaves and other bits on top of soil. One old leaf might have 1,000 tiny mites chewing it to bits. Mites like to feed when the weather is cool and damp. When the sun comes out, they crawl down into the soil. They will die if they get too warm and dry.

17

MT. LEBANON PUBLIC LIBRARY

# Wriggly Rotters

Some of the best rotters are worms. There are many different kinds of worms. Big earthworms can grow as long as a person's arm. Some roundworms, or nematodes, are too small to see. Most of these worms eat almost any dead thing they can find. Some worms wriggle through soil, while others burrow into dead animals and plants.

An earthworm has no eyes or ears at its head end—just a round mouth that swallows tiny pieces of soil.

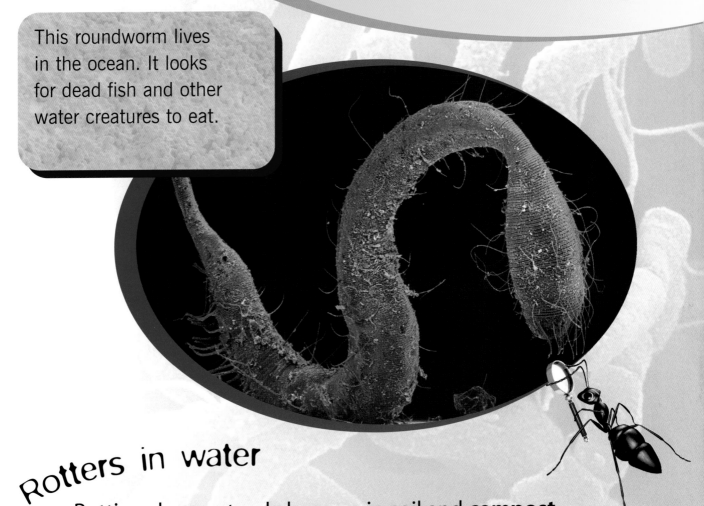

**LONGEST WORMS**

Ribbonworms live on the seashore. They scavenge (eat dead parts of animals). They are the longest worms. Some are more than 100 feet (30 meters) long!

This roundworm lives in the ocean. It looks for dead fish and other water creatures to eat.

## Rotters in water

Rotting does not only happen in soil and **compost heaps**. It also happens on the bottom of ponds, rivers, lakes, and the oceans. Water-living worms burrow into the bodies of dead creatures such as fish and even whales, and eat them to pieces.

# Living by Rotting

Molds can grow almost anywhere. If you leave fruit for too long in a bowl, it goes **moldy**. Even vegetables on a shelf, clothes in a damp closet, and damp paper can go moldy.

This fruit has gone rotten from the middle outward. The rings on its skin are called pinmolds.

Molds grow on the plaster on damp walls and ceilings, forming dark patches.

# Old and moldy

Molds are living things called **fungi**. All fungi live by rotting plant or animal material. They get their food by making special substances that eat into living or dead things, turning them into a liquid. The hungry fungus then soaks up this liquid. As the fungus does this, it speeds rot and **decay**. There are thousands of kinds of fungi. You can read more about them on the next page.

**A LOT OF NAMES**
There are lots of names for different kinds of fungi. There are molds, pinmolds, mildews, rusts, blights, yeasts, mushrooms, toadstools—and lots more!

# Threads of Decay

Molds and other **fungi** cause most of the world's rotting. They make dead things rot until there is nothing left. They do this by growing tiny threads that are usually too thin to see. The threads eat their way into dead bits of plants and animals. Then the threads turn them into a liquid, and soak it up as food.

Dry rot is a fungus that grows through wood. It makes the wood **decay** into a powder.

**A LOT OF THREADS**
If you could take all the threads of a fungus from a cupful of soil, and join them end to end, they could stretch more than 320 feet (100 meters).

The threads of a fungus form a tangled net in the soil, like a spider's web.

## Killer fungi

Some kinds of fungi spread through the soil. If their threads touch an old leaf or an animal dropping, they grow around it and into it, and rot it. Sometimes they grow into living things, such as trees, flowers, or sick animals, and do the same. This is when fungi are not only rotters—they are killers, too.

**Fungi** are the world's best rotters. This is partly because they spread themselves so fast. The main part of a fungus is its tangled net of tiny threads. But in some places, the threads grow into larger parts, called fruiting bodies. In many kinds of fungus, these are quite big. We call the fruiting bodies mushrooms or toadstools.

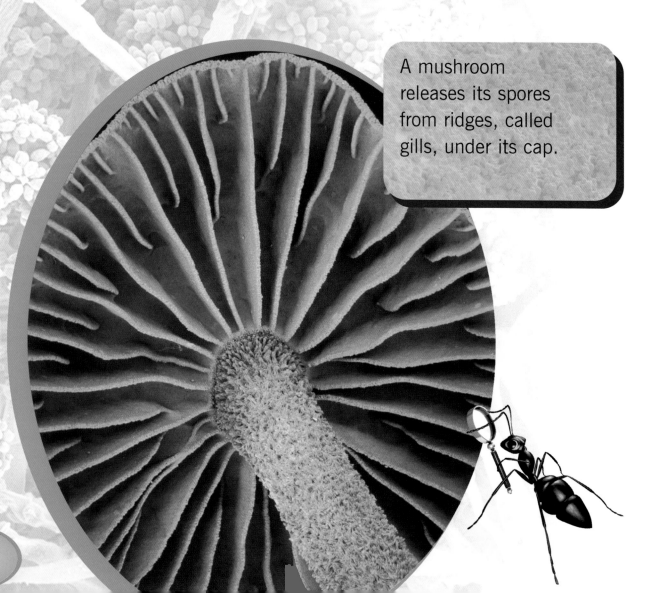

A mushroom releases its spores from ridges, called gills, under its cap.

One spore from a fungus is too small to see. But millions together look like a powdery cloud, floating away from this earthstar fungus.

## How fungi spread

Mushrooms and toadstools can be bigger than a dinner plate or smaller than a pin's head. They make seedlike **spores**, which are much too small to see. The spores float away in the wind. If the spores land in a suitable damp place, they grow into new fungi. This is how fungi spread.

**PUFF, PUFF**
**A puffball is a round fungus, the size of a soccer ball. It can puff out as many as 20 billion tiny spores!**

# Smallest Rotters

As things rot, they break into smaller pieces, which are eaten by tinier creatures. Smallest of all are two kinds of microlife—protists and **bacteria**. Protists are Jell-O-like blobs that slide along, taking in any bits of food. Bacteria are even smaller living things—about 1,000 would fit on the dot of this "i." They soak up almost any kind of juicy rotten food.

This kind of protist is called an amoeba. It has a lot of bendy arms, which wave around to catch tiny pieces of food.

**ROTTERS WE EAT**
People can eat some fungi, from ordinary mushrooms to potato-shaped **truffles**. But other fungi are poisonous. We must be sure which kind they are.

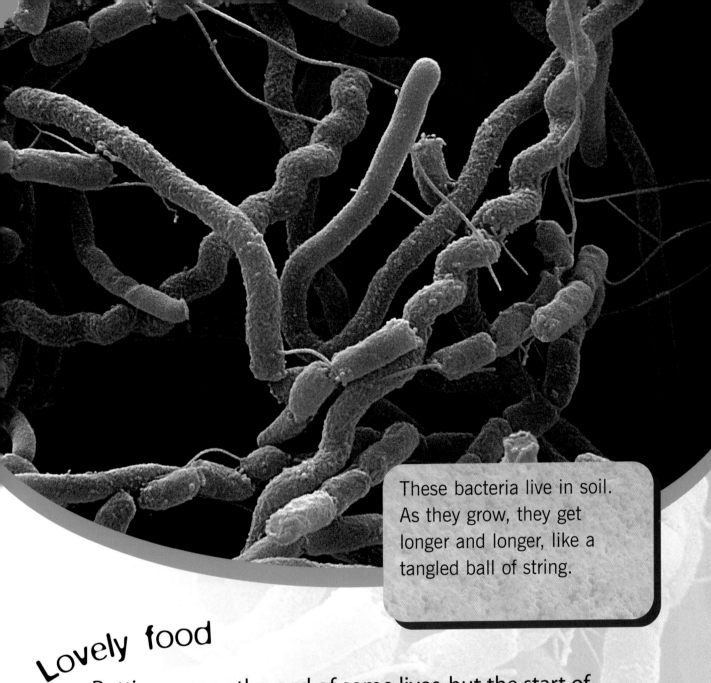

These bacteria live in soil. As they grow, they get longer and longer, like a tangled ball of string.

## Lovely food

Rotting means the end of some lives, but the start of others. Tiny bacteria, protists, **fungi**, and minibeasts get their food from making other things rot. Then they become food, too. These rotters are eaten by centipedes, spiders, and many other animals. Then these small animals are eaten by larger animals. This is how rotting becomes nature's way of recycling.

# Stop the Rot!

Rotting can ruin our farm crops, fruit, vegetables, and meat. It can also damage the wood in our furniture and houses. Rot happens faster in warm and damp places. To try to stop things from rotting, we keep them cool and dry. Refrigerators slow down rot, because they are cold. Freezers can almost stop it completely.

If our foods stay too warm and damp, like these heads of lettuce, they soon go **moldy**.

# Why we need rot

People try to stop rot in some places. But in nature, rot is very important. It gets rid of old, dead plants and animals. It recycles (reuses) their tiniest parts into soil. Then new plants can grow and animals can eat the plants. We all depend on microlife that rots things.

## CLEANING AWAY ROTTERS

Keeping things clean and dry helps to stop **decay**. It removes the tiny **spores** of **fungi** and other rotters, which float in air and hide in dirt.

Chemicals called **fungicides** stop molds from growing. Farmers sometimes spray their crops with them.

# Find Out for Yourself

## More Books to Read

Bial, Raymond. *A Handful of Dirt*. New York, N.Y.: Walker & Company, 2000.

Burnie, David. *Inside Guides: Microlife*. New York, N.Y.: Dorling Kindersley Family Library, 1997.

Moseley, Keith, and Andy Everitt-Stewart. *The Things in Mouldy Manor* New York, N.Y.: Grosset & Dunlap, 1994.

Pfeffer, E. Wendy, and Robin Brickman. *A Log's Life*. Riverside, N.J.: Simon & Schuster Children's Publishing, 1997.

Portman, Michelle Eva. *Compost, By Gosh!* Warner, N.H.: Flower Press, 2002.

## Using the Internet

Explore the Internet to find out more about microlife that rots things. Use a search engine and type in a keyword such as fungus, mold, termite, or compost, or the name of a particular type of microlife.

# Glossary

**bacteria**  tiny living things. Some bacteria make things rot.

**compost heap**  pile of dead plant material such as leaves, grass cuttings, and vegetable peelings

**conifer**  type of tree that grows cones rather than flowers, such as a pine or fir tree

**decay**  break apart and become rotten or moldy

**fungi**  group of living things including mushrooms, toadstools, and yeasts. Fungi cause rotting.

**fungicides**  substances that kill fungi

**grub**  a baby beetle that looks like a worm

**leaf litter**  mixture of dead leaves, bits of twigs, and loose soil found under trees

**maggot**  young or larva of a fly. Maggots do not have legs.

**microscope**  equipment to make very small things look bigger

**mite**  small, eight-legged creature. Some mites cause disease and some are harmless to people.

**moldy**  going bad or becoming rotten due to mold, a type of fungus

**spores**  tiny, seedlike parts that are made by fungi. Spores grow into new fungi.

**truffle**  type of potato-shaped fungi that grows underground

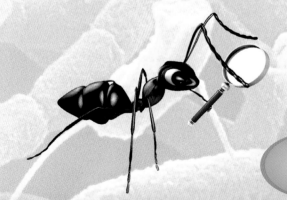

# Index

MT. LEBANON PUBLIC LIBRARY

MT. LEBANON PUBLIC LIBRARY